EMANUEL SWEDENBORG (1688-1772) is today acknowledged as one of the great thinkers of the eighteenth century and a pioneering figure in the history of Western thought. Philosopher, theologian, visionary, scientist and statesman, his book *Heaven and Hell* has had a direct influence on William Blake, Honoré de Balzac, W B Yeats, S T Coleridge, Fyodor Dostoevsky, Helen Keller, C G Jung and many others, and his theory of correspondences is rightly understood as one of the defining influences on Romantic and Symbolist thought. More recently, through the work of Czeslaw Milosz, Italo Calvino, A S Byatt and Iain Sinclair, we see his name re-emerge in relation to 'pyschogeography', 'historical realism' and 'magical realism'. Jorge Luis Borges once described him as the most extraordinary man in recorded history.

STEPHEN MCNEILLY is a writer, artist, curator, anthologist and museum director at Swedenborg House, London. He is also the series editor of the *Swedenborg Archive Series* and the *Journal of the Swedenborg Society*, the latter described by Annalisa Volpone as a 'mapping of the impact of Swedenborg's thought on the western literary imaginaire'. Recent books include *Philosophy, Mysticism, Literature: an anthology of essays on Emanuel Swedenborg* (2013) and *Swedenborg's Lusthus* (2024).

Concerning an idea about place

Concerning an idea about place

SWEDENBORG'S SUMMERHOUSE

STEPHEN MCNEILLY

SWEDENBORG HOUSE
LONDON

2024

LIMITED EDITION 200

———

200

CONCERNING AN IDEA ABOUT
PLACE: SWEDENBORG'S SUMMERHOUSE
© 2024, STEPHEN MCNEILLY

COVER AND BOOK DESIGN © 2024, THE QUINN FIZZLERS

Published by:
The Swedenborg Society
Swedenborg House
20-21 Bloomsbury Way
London WC1A 2TH

ISBN: 978-0-85448-229-0
British Library Cataloguing-in-Publication Data.
A catalogue record for this book
is available from the British Library.

Contents

Preliminary note

Part reliquary, part sanctum and part tourist attraction, Swedenborg's summerhouse has long been an object of pilgrimage and curiosity. Built as a wooden retreat at the far end of his garden in Stockholm in 1747 and serving as a focal point for his writing and otherworldly conversations, it has since become emblematic of a certain type of thinking and also of a certain type of writing. Today it sits in Skansen, the open-air museum in Stockholm, and has been an inspiration for writers and artists for over 200 years.

Drawing on a long-standing engagement with Swedenborg's writing on place and time, the essay printed here is intended to accompany the exhibition *Swedenborg's Lusthus* staged in two chapters at Swedenborg House, London, in 2024.[1] An early version of this essay was published in *Swedenborg's Lusthus* (2024), an anthology of texts and images including contributions from Chloe Arijdis, Daniel Birnbaum, Anonymous Bosch, Deborah Levy, Iain Sinclair and

Ken Worpole amongst others: both exhibition and essay exploring the cultural and historical impact of this small garden hut.[2]

For their comments and generosity I would like to thank Daniel Cartwright, Anya Reeve, Adam Skipper, James Wilson and the team at Swedenborg House. Acknowledgements must also be extended to the Nordiska Museet and the Stadsmuseet in Stockholm. In addition to the book just mentioned, readers interested in finding out more about Swedenborg are directed to *Introducing Swedenborg*,[3] a concise biography by Peter Ackroyd and *Philosophy, Literature, Mysticism: an Anthology of Essays on the Thought and Influence of Emanuel Swedenborg* including contributions by Czeslaw Milosz amongst others.[4]

Stephen McNeilly, 2024

NOTES

1 *Swedenborg's Lusthus,* Swedenborg House, curated by Stephen McNeilly, (London, 2024).

2 Stephen McNeilly (ed), *Swedenborg's Lusthus*, with Foreword by Deborah Levy (London: Swedenborg Society, 2024).

3 Peter Ackroyd, *Introducing Swedenborg* (London: Swedenborg Society, 2021).

4 Stephen McNeilly (ed), *Philosophy, Literature, Mysticism: an Anthology of Essays on the Thought and Influence of Emanuel Swedenborg* (London: Swedenborg Society, 2013); expanded edition forthcoming in 2025.

Chronology

1688   Born Emanuel Swedberg on January 29.

1709   Swedberg graduates from Uppsala University and publishes his dissertation under the title *Selected Sentences*.

1710-15 Swedberg travels to London and attends lectures at the Royal Society where Isaac Newton is President. He studies under Edmond Halley and John Flamsteed and drafts designs for a series of inventions—including a water clock and a submarine, which have since become lost—and during his return journey to Sweden publishes 3 volumes of poetry entitled *Ludus Heliconius*, *Festivus Applausus* and *Camena Borea*.

1716-18 Through Christopher Polhem he is introduced to King Charles XII of Sweden and publishes *Daedalus Hyperboreus*, Sweden's first scientific journal. He declines an invitation to become

Professor of Mathematics at Uppsala University and publishes Sweden's first textbook on Algebra. He publishes the first of a series of texts in which he attempts to solve the question of longitude by means of the moon.

1719 The Swedberg family are ennobled by Queen Ulrika Eleanora resulting in a change of name for Emanuel to Swedenborg. With this honour comes a peerage and Swedenborg takes a seat in the Swedish House of Nobles.

1722-4 Swedenborg publishes *Miscellaneous Observations*, pts 1, 2, 3 and 4, plus a short work on Swedish coinage. He receives an important salaried position as Assessor on the Swedish Board of Mines and declines an invitation to succeed Nils Celsius as Professor of Astronomy at Uppsala University.

1734 Swedenborg publishes his three-volume philosophical and scientific *magnum opus* entitled *Opera Philosophica et Mineralia*. This is accompanied by *On the Infinite and The Final Cause of Creation/The Mechanism of the Operation of the Soul and the Body*. He receives international renown and is invited to open a correspondence with the Russian Academy of Sciences. He visits Leipzig at the same time as J S Bach but there is no record of them having met.

1735   Swedenborg's father, Bishop Jesper Swedberg, dies. Carl Linnaeus, Swedenborg's cousin by marriage, publishes *Systema Naturæ* which includes his now famous taxonomy of the animal kingdom entitled *Regnum Animale*.

1736-8 Swedenborg begins a study of the brain resulting in two large unpublished manuscripts entitled *The Cerebrum* and *The Brain*.

1740-1 Swedenborg is nominated into the Royal Swedish Academy of Sciences by Linnaeus and publishes his *Oeconomia Regni Animalis,* described later by R W Emerson as 'one of those books which, by the sustained dignity of thinking, is an honor to the human race'.

1743-4 Swedenborg buys a house and plot of land in Hornsgatan, Stockholm, from the City Treasurer Carl Segerlund for 6,000 dalars, and then travels to Holland to publish his *Regnum Animale*. In a private journal, published after his death as the *Journal of Dreams*, he describes having a vision of Christ in Delft. When in Holland he publishes parts 1 and 2 of his *Regnum Animale* and then moves to London to publish part 3. Shortly after he receives a 'heavenly commission' to write about his spiritual experiences.

1745   He publishes *The Worship and Love of God* and then returns to Stockholm and takes up

residence in his former rented lodgings on
Räntmästarehuset owned by Linnaeus. He
begins an in-depth study of the Hebrew Bible
and drafts a multi-volume study of the Old
Testament entitled *The Word Explained*, both of
which are left unpublished.

1746-7 He moves into the property on Hornsgatan
and the summerhouse is built shortly after. He
begins writing of his daily visionary experiences
in a private journal published after his death as
The Spiritual Diary. Immersed in his visionary
experiences he resigns from his role as Assessor
from the Board of Mines and leaves Stockholm
for Holland. He makes reference to his
'lusthuset' in a notebook.

1748 When drafting volume one of *Arcana Coelestia*
he makes a second reference to his *'lusthuset'*
in a notebook that contains the list of materials
needed for its construction.

1749-56 He publishes *Arcana Coelestia*, which he
has printed anonymously in 8 volumes, over
a period of 7 years. In 1753 Carl Linnaeus
publishes *Species Plantarum* and in 1755
Europe is shocked by the Lisbon earthquake.

1757-9 When in London, Swedenborg writes of a
'Last Judgment' in the spiritual world, the date
of which coincides with the birth of William

Blake. In 1758 he publishes five works drawn from his eight-volume *Arcana Coelestia*. In English, these works are later published as *Worlds in Space*, *The Last Judgment*, *The New Jerusalem and Its Heavenly Teaching*, *The White Horse* and *Heaven and Hell*, his most popular work. He prepares for the press a multi-volume commentary on the Book of Revelation entitled *The Apocalypse Explained* but decides, for reasons still unknown, not to publish it. Voltaire publishes *Candide*.

1762   Jean-Jacques Rousseau publishes *Emile, or On Education*.

1763-4 Swedenborg travels to Amsterdam and publishes 5 new works, namely *On the New Jerusalem concerning the Lord*, *On the New Jerusalem concerning Sacred Scripture*, *On the New Jerusalem concerning Life*, *On the New Jerusalem concerning Faith* and *Continuation on the Last Judgment and the Spiritual World*. These are printed by François Changuion, sometime publisher of Voltaire. Immanuel Kant writes to Swedenborg and Swedenborg indicates he will offer a reply in a forthcoming work. *Divine Love and Wisdom* is published soon after in Amsterdam. Samuel Johnson meets James Boswell in London. In 1764

Swedenborg publishes *Divine Providence.*

1766-7 Immanuel Kant publishes his book on
Swedenborg which is later translated into
English as *Dreams of a Spirit-Seer.* Swedenborg
publishes an exegesis of the Book of Revelation
entitled *The Apocalypse Revealed.* 1767 sees the
premiere of Wolfgang Amadeus Mozart's first
opera *Apollo et Hyacinthus,* in Salzburg.

1768-9 In 1768 Swedenborg publishes *Conjugial
Love* and for the first time puts his name on
the title page of one of his theological works.
The following year he publishes *A Brief
Description of the Teachings of the New Church*
and *The Interaction of the Soul and Body,* and
controversy breaks out in Sweden regarding the
publication of *Conjugial Love.* In Sweden his
books are confiscated.

1770 Swedenborg makes an appeal to King Adolf
Frederic regarding the controversy and the
subsequent charge of heresy.

1771 Swedenborg travels to Amsterdam and publishes
his last great work, *The True Christian Religion*
and then makes his final journey to London.
When in London he lodges at the home of
Richard Shearsmith in Clerkenwell and suffers
from a stroke but partially recovers.

1772 He corresponds briefly with John Wesley and

on Sunday 29 March at 4pm, he dies. His body is interred in the crypt at the Swedish Church in Princes Square, Wapping. Back in Stockholm, his estate and library are put up for auction and the house and garden are sold. The property is divided into three separate lots and visitors from overseas begin to visit the summerhouse.

1789-94 William Blake produces a series of Swedenborg-inspired poems, including his famous *Songs of Innocence and Experience* and *The Marriage of Heaven and Hell*. At this time, and spurred by rumours that Swedenborg's body was no longer in the crypt, his coffin is opened twice, in quick succession.

1816 Swedenborg's coffin was opened once more and his skull was stolen by the phrenologist John Didrik Holm. Holm returns the wrong skull which in turn is stolen from the crypt in 1817.

1832-4 Honoré de Balzac publishes his Swedenborg-inspired novellas *Louis Lambert* and *Séraphîta*.

1850 R W Emerson publishes his famous essay on Swedenborg in *Representative Men*.

1853 The first illustrated publication of the summerhouse and the property at Hornsgatan is published by J S Hobson in London, which references a description and visit by William

Wilkinson, then Secretary of the Swedenborg Society, London.

1857 Charles Baudelaire publishes *Les Fleurs du mal*, which includes the Swedenborg-inspired poem 'Correpondances'.

1866-8 An appeal for funds is published in the Swedenborgian periodical the *Intellectual Repository* for the upkeep, preservation and repair of the summerhouse. Soon after the main dwelling in Hornsgatan is torn down.

1891-5 The summerhouse is occupied by the sculptor Richard Sundell who installs a life size waxwork of Swedenborg in a coffin and covers the walls with 'black cloth covered with silver stars'. Sundell introduces an entrance fee of 25 ore.

1896 The summerhouse is purchased by Arthur Hazelius and moved to Skansen on 26 February.

1908 Swedenborg's remains, including the wrong skull, are removed from the crypt in Wapping and returned to Sweden with state ceremony and are placed in a sealed sarcophagus at Uppsala Cathedral.

1924 Alongside Dante, Hegel, Rimbaud and others, Swedenborg's name is cited as a source of inspiration in André Breton's *Surrealist Manifesto*.

1957   Swedenborg's real skull is discovered in
        Swansea and the discovery inspires the Welsh
        poet Vernon Watkins to write a poem about it.
1964   The summerhouse is moved from its original
        site behind Bergsman's Garden in Skansen to
        the Rose Garden where it still rests.
1978   A replica summerhouse is built in Hornsgatan,
        the original site of Swedenborg's house and
        property. The same year, Swedenborg's real
        skull is put up for auction at Sotheby's and
        soon after interred with his remains at Uppsala.
2006   The Swedenborg manuscripts, held at the
        Royal Academy of Sciences in Stockholm, are
        designated as part of UNESCO's World Memory
        programme.
2008   A second replica summerhouse is built at the
        Swedenborg Memorial Church, Tegnérlunden,
        Stockholm.

The state of each spirit is known from the place in which they dwell [...] for all live in a place that corresponds with their state, i.e., not only from the neighbourhood but also of the distance of that neighbourhood from the centre of the city. Spirits are also known from the various gatherings and assemblies in which they attend, and something similar can also be seen from the position of a seat within a house: for each spirit knows his or her own seat in a room and is known by it, [...] and each go to that part of the house which corresponds to their state.

—Swedenborg

Our soul is an abode. And by remembering
'houses and 'rooms' we learn to abide within
ourselves. —Gaston Bachelard [1]

The natural assumption when speaking of writing and place, writes Seamus Heaney in *Finders Keepers*, is to view the poet or writer as standing in some expressive or interpretive relationship to the milieu. The voice of the author merges into the landscape as an outward sign of an inner sensibility and the 'scene of writing' becomes a 'locus of energy'. [2] Heaney is speaking in particular of Thoor Ballylee, the fifteenth-century Norman keep in County Galway where W B Yeats lived and wrote his now famous poems, but the metaphor holds good for a number of writers and literary dwellings. We might think of Henry David Thoreau's small hut at Walden

Pond, Ludwig Wittgenstein's cabin in Norway,
or Virginia Woolf's shed in Rodmell, Sussex.
In each there is foregrounded a relationship
between writer and the spirit of place in which
the posture of the building creates 'touchstones
for the work', or as Heaney writes of Thoor
Ballylee, the tower forms a symbolic focal point
where 'utterance and being' might be said to
dwell and coalesce. [3]

The small summerhouse, now housed at
Skansen, the open-air museum in Stockholm,
and the 'scene of writing' of Swedenborg's late
visionary works, might be viewed as another
such 'locus of energy'. Shed, hut, study, portal,
sanctum, retreat and 'antenna chamber', the
building served as a place of study and quiet
contemplation for over two decades. Designed
and constructed at a time when Swedenborg
first began documenting his spiritual
experiences, it was here that he recorded
his conversations with the eminent dead—
including Aristotle, Melanchthon, Newton, St

Paul and numerous others—and it was here that
Swedenborg wrote the majority of his visionary
works, including *Heaven and Hell*, *Divine
Love and Wisdom*, *Conjugial Love*, *The True
Christian Religion* and others. Commissioned
by the author himself it is likewise the only
outpost still standing that bears witness to the
uncommon story of Swedenborg's late visionary
experiences and also to his writing on place.

Historians of early church architecture
have long emphasized the role of the 'cell' as
providing a shrine or temple to the interior
life, [4] and as far back as the ninth century BC,
in a story well-known to Swedenborg, there
is the example of Elisha, the prophet, whose
holiness is framed by a small chamber which,
like the *lusthus*, contained a bed, a table, a
stool, and a candlestick. 'Let us make a little
chamber, I pray thee, on the wall: and let us set
for him there a bed, a table, and a stool, and a
candlestick'. (2 Kings 4:10.) For William Blake,
some 40 years after Swedenborg's last visit to

London, this chamber is envisioned as a frame within a frame, a sacred space or sanctuary into which the prophet enters and is changed: he is transformed from an object of the world into an object of thought and interiority. [5]

At stake is the question of the spatiality of thought and the degree to which dwelling and being are determined by our sense of identity and place. In the case of Swedenborg and the summerhouse we might view this firstly in the type of thinking and writing that occurred there. But secondly, we may also encounter this less directly through the imprint or traces of the author's spatial sovereignty, that is of viewing the summerhouse as a symbolic edifice or simulacra corresponding to the author's internal acoustics.

*

My own interest in the summerhouse began in the summer of 1991. Having spent most of the spring reading Swedenborg's multi-volume *Arcana Caelestia* in parallel with his *Spiritual*

Diary, I drifted off to sleep one afternoon and found myself standing in a field in front of a small wooden hut. Framed by a double set of doors, I looked inside and caught sight of a straw bed, a wooden table and chair, oak floorboards but most impressively, on the back wall, an entrance doorway to an inner chamber covered with a veil. On waking I made a pencil sketch.

Since then and having visited the house in person on numerous occasions, the experience has confirmed a common perception of the hut as a site embodying Swedenborg's own oneiric or otherworldly visitations, and also as a site of multiple identities and multiple representations. Today, in fact, there are three summerhouses. In addition to the original hut at Skansen, the open-air museum in Stockholm, a second full-scale replica sits in Hornsgatan, the place of Swedenborg's home, and a third smaller reconstruction is located in the courtyard of the *Nya Kyrkans Församling* in Stockholm.

Each bear witness to the uncommon legacy of Swedenborg's thought, and each in their own way serves as a 'touchstone' for our own desires and retellings. Indeed, when standing inside the *lusthus* looking out, one encounters the world as a simulation. Time itself becomes fragmented, and so also our relationship with the outside.

'To Hultman [...] while I think of it, will you please not light a fire in the lusthus stove, as the chimney in the loft is open underneath, and sparks could enter and ignite the papers there, where I have stored them, and other things; besides, there is no need for a fire to be lit there'. [6] This draft note of a letter by Swedenborg occurs in a private journal dated January 1748 when Swedenborg was in Holland and is prefigured in an aide memoir written several months previously in November 1747. [7]

From the standpoint of dating, the note is especially important as it represents only one of two occasions in which Swedenborg mentions the lusthus directly by name. He left Stockholm for Holland on 24 July 1747 having moved into the property in the spring of 1746. [8] This would place the construction of the summerhouse to sometime between the summer of 1746 and the spring of 1747. It was also during this time that Swedenborg began recording his spiritual experiences.

The second reference comes in another manuscript notebook and is mostly likely dated around 1746. This reference includes a list of materials and costs for its construction. Items on the list include:

> *80 beams of hard wood;*
> *12 loads of pine planks;*
> *25 loads for boards.*

We also see costings for

> *doors;*
> *windows;*

hinges;
locks,
nails;
roof slating;
and a wood burning stove.

To this Swedenborg adds calculations for a glass fitter, a plasterer and workmen. The total expenditure is given as 2232 dalars, around one third of the price of the entire property. [9]

We do not know to what degree Swedenborg himself was involved in the design and construction of the hut but we see no outlay here for an architect or head contractor. As a gifted structural engineer Swedenborg would have had no difficulties working directly with the tradesmen in laying the foundations and overseeing the design.

From the auction catalogue for the sale of the property [10] we also learn that Swedenborg attached a small garden tool shed to the rear at the right, and a room for his library at the rear to the left. Inside, the hut was sparsely furnished, hosting a desk, chairs and oil lamps. The interior walls were painted a deep viridian green on hessian wall covering.

From other sources we are told that he kept a straw mattress in the recess at the rear during the summer months and his maid once made mention of a full-length mirror out of which Swedenborg is later said to have seen the visions that 'float[ed] towards him'. [11] The addition of a small wood burning stove indicates that Swedenborg likewise used the hut during the winter and autumn months. It would have also been used to keep his coffee warm, for himself and for visitors. In the attic he stored his manuscript papers. This we see in the draft letter to Hultman, written not long after the building had been constructed.

Interestingly, of Hultman himself we hear almost nothing more and he rarely features in the story of Swedenborg's biography. Based in Stockholm, we learn only that he served as

Swedenborg's financial advisor for nearly 30 years, between 1737 to 1764.

*

In addition to these two direct mentions there is also a third reference or allusion written by Swedenborg in 1748, around one year after these early notes, and drafted when Swedenborg was in lodgings in London. This reference is perhaps the most significant in that it draws attention to an otherwise overlooked connection between the hut and his newly developing visionary experiences. We also find here an interesting shift in his use of terminology:

> *I have sometimes, in my sleep, observed that in my garden in Stockholm there were various rooms of doves near the earth with stone entrances, enclosures and chambers* [camerae] *of beautiful construction within, and I wondered that there were such things in my garden and yet I had not known it.*

*Also, at a different height to which it was
necessary to ascend by ladders, there was
seen something similar, and on a third
elevation there were shepherds, meadows
and groves. Last night I also had a vivid
perception in a dream of a house* [mansio]
*near the earth in a garden in which I saw a
room with a tenant, and with whom I spoke.
On awaking I spoke with the spirits around
me, who answered me as if they themselves
were also in the dream. Near the earth were
artisans with whom a conversation was
held concerning a census.* [12]

Frustratingly, Swedenborg does not decipher
the dream as he does of other dreams
elsewhere in this work but in his vast system of
correspondences doves are given to represent
those ideas and affections we have that are
related to regeneration, [13] whilst a garden
corresponds to intelligence or the general
ground on which our ideas are framed or

formed. [14] In this case we see that the various 'chambers' within the garden rise upwards into three 'elevations', one for each tier of the mind.

Key also to an understanding of this passage is Swedenborg's use of the terms *mansiones* and *camerae*. In Latin *mansio* and *camera* are used primarily to denote private chambers or rooms, personalized dwellings like a bedroom or the chambers of Noah's ark, where the passage of time is measured against a task at hand. From the latter we have terms such as *camera obscura* and *camera lucida*. Elsewhere Swedenborg contrasts this with the term *domus* (house) which he uses to symbolize the whole mind, or a person in total.

In his *Divine Love and Wisdom*, for instance, Swedenborg writes that because the mind corresponds to the body, by house (*domus*) is meant the whole body, including the 'members, organs, and viscera'. [15] *Domus* representing a home for the soul, an archetype of no fixed time or the place in which Being resides. A *mansio* or *camera*, in contrast, denotes a personalized inner space or a portal, or a place of transition through which thought might ascend.

S wedenborg purchased the land on Hornsgatan from the City Treasurer, Carl Segerlund on 26 March 1743. It cost 6,000 dalars, which he paid for in copper cash, and was situated in a semi-rural village just south of the city centre. [16] His neighbour to the east was the grocer Kempe, and to the west the rope-maker Nyman. The Church of St Mary Magdalene stood some 500 metres due west and just a short walk along Hornsgatan was the residence of his former mentor, and one-time collaborator, Christopher Polhem.

Having previously lodged in rented accommodation—the most recent being a two-roomed apartment in the fashionable block

of Räntmästarehuset, once inhabited by his
cousin Carl Linnaeus—Hornsgatan was the
first property that Swedenborg had bought for
himself, the purchase coinciding with the first
payment of his pension, awarded by Royal
Assent for 20 years' service as Assessor of the
Royal Board of Mines. Three months later, on 21
July 1743, he left Stockholm for Holland.

In a letter to the king requesting a leave
of absence from the Royal Board of Mines,
Swedenborg writes of his intention to produce
a large philosophico-anatomical work in Latin
entitled *Regnum Animale*, an extension of an
earlier multi-volume work entitled *Oeconomia
Regni Animalis*. [17] Both were an attempt to
trace a map of the body as 'the whole world or
microcosm which the soul inhabits'. [18] Parts I &
II of the *Regnum Animale* were published in
The Hague a year later, in 1744. On his way to
Holland Swedenborg kept by his side a pocket-
sized journal—bound in parchment—containing
fifty-four leaves of crowded text in Swedish.

Among the many descriptions of places and people, he began recounting his dreams, and made special mention of one event in particular, dated 6 April.

Alone in his lodgings, he describes an encounter with the image of Christ. [19] Three weeks later he set sail for London and settled for a time in Salisbury Court off Fleet Street, but the dreams continued, or rather they turn into visions, and from his diary we have an account of an intense inner transformation. Towards the end of his life, when describing a key moment in this process to his friend Carl Robsahm, he recalls the following episode:

> *I was in London and had dinner somewhat late in the cellar vaults of a restaurant where I used to eat, and had a chamber by myself, where I amused myself with thoughts on the just mentioned subject. I was hungry and ate with a good appetite. Towards the end of the meal I noticed*

something like dimness before my eyes,
it darkened and I saw the floor covered
with the most hideous crawling animals,
like snakes, frogs and such creatures. I
was startled, because I was completely
conscious and my comprehension was
rational; eventually darkness prevailed,
but suddenly it was dispelled and I saw a
man sitting in one corner of the chamber.
Since I was then all alone I was quite
amazed when he started talking and
said to me: 'Do not eat so much'. Again it
darkened before my eyes but soon cleared
up quickly, and then I found myself alone
in the room.

That evening the man appeared once again and revealed himself as 'the Lord God, the creator and redeemer of the world'. [20]

On his return to Stockholm sixteen months later Swedenborg lodged initially in the two-room apartment in the Räntmästarehuset. To

family, colleagues and friends he appeared
unchanged but in private he began preparations
for his most ambitious work to date, a multi-
volume biblical exegesis unfolding the inner
meaning of each chapter, verse and word
of Genesis and Exodus. In this he outlined
the blueprint of his own experience and the
framework for his future theology. It was in
this notebook also that he drafted the list of
raw provisions for the summerhouse containing
wood, glass, slate, stone and a small wood
burning stove.

In private almanacs of the period we also
see him document rare seeds and flowers for
the garden, many of which were purchased for
him from the New World by his Dutch friend
and agent Joachim Wretman. [21] In front of the
main house he kept a small garden where he
cultivated a vegetable patch and topiary bushes
cut into the shape of animals and other things
in the 'Dutch fashion'. Within the property there
was also a carriage house and small barn for his

cows, and a vaulted cellar to keep his produce fresh. At the far end of the garden he planted a small orchard. He also had constructed a maze or labyrinth and a small mirror house at the centre for entertaining visitors, modelled on a version seen on a visit to an English country house. Perhaps most importantly, he built a covered walkway from the main house to the summerhouse, which passed through the library. And immediately in front of the hut he planted two poplar trees and built a small house for the keeping of doves.

R eaders familiar with Swedenborg's theory of correspondence will be aware of the claim that objects and signs are outward reflections of inner impulses: the world unfolds before us like a living, hieroglyphic text, a theatre giving spatiality and temporality to our thoughts and affections. The measure of the thought being equal to the ratio of our environs—the one fitting into the other like a hand inside a glove. We are 'justified in believing that the whole world is filled with types', writes Swedenborg in his *Hieroglyphic Key* of 1744, 'but we understand very few of them'. [22] The future and the past form a symbolic chain in which space is embedded in our relationship with the present, and so also of place. Elsewhere Swedenborg calls this relation a representation of 'state', and it serves as a foundation or terminus within which our ideas and affections can be formulated and find rest. The one giving form and shape to the other.

'I have spoken frequently with spirits about the idea of place and distance', Swedenborg adds at §1376 of his *Arcana Caelestia*,

> *and with them they are not anything real being nothing other than their states of thought and affection which vary in the way place and distance do and which visually present themselves as such in the world of spirits. This is not so much the case with angels in heaven. They have no idea of place or of time, but only of states.* [23]

In the highest of the heavens the representations and conditions of place remain relatively constant because each angel is governed by a similar 'ruling love' or primary affection. A continuity of form is established through a community of shared loves. But in the lower heavens, or the spiritual world, abrupt changes of place can often occur because there is a greater divergence in the collective affections of the spirits there. In this way a spirit's location is often pulled and pushed in uncertain ways and an indeterminacy is introduced according to the intentionality of the spirits present.

In such a way also—or when seen in reverse—can the quality of each spirit or angel be ascertained by the quality or attributes of the place in which they are standing or dwelling. In one passage of his *Spiritual Diary* Swedenborg even observes that every spirit 'knows his seat in a room and is known from it' and goes 'to that part of a house which corresponds' to their quality. [24] And Swedenborg himself notes that having spent time in one room of his lodgings 'it became familiar to me so that I could then better command my ideas', whereas in another room the spirits with him became confused and disorientated and he was not able to write:

> *yesterday, having removed from the room where I was sitting to another adjoining room, [...] a kind of tranquillity ensued among the spirits [with me], though ignorant, as it were, of where I was, at which I wondered. I am now speaking of the fact, that spirits wish to have their ideas connected with place, as unless (the place is) at the same time in their idea, things have a kind of foreign air to them, and they know not, as it were, where they are, so that the idea is not determinate unless it relates to place. It was moreover observed that one place has a preference (in their esteem) over another, especially from the vicinity of spirits who seem to themselves to be conversant there, as might be abundantly confirmed by facts, besides that the same effect is produced by the presence of men who are near, and in the house.* [25]

'The ground of all this', he adds, is that our
ideas are 'not finited (or fixed) without space,
or which is the same thing, without structure
(or form)', hence for spirits, places and material
things serve 'as fulcra on which (their thoughts)
stand'. [26] In our natural world the emphasis
is weighted towards the materiality of things
because experience is governed by the
appearance that thought is determined by place
and not the reverse. But this is an illusion of
the senses. In the heavens the dwellings of the
angels are always representative of their inner
state and they are beautiful beyond compare.

In one vision this is confirmed with an image
of 'porticoes or vaulted [...] galleries' where
one could stroll within walls decorated with
'marvellously woven garlands of flowers besides
many other decorations which [...] change and
replace one another'. They were sometimes seen
in a brighter or dimmer light, but always with
'interior delight'. As extensions of the angels that
dwell within them, they change and become

more beautiful as an angel grows in perfection, and when this occurs 'something like a window appears on the side'. [27]

In another it is represented by a visitation from the protestant theologian Philip Melanchthon who is seen by Swedenborg oscillating between two rooms, one with a panelled ceiling and the other a cold, stone cellar underneath a judge:

> *When dwelling in the panelled room he is clothed in furs like bearskins, and in this way is protected from the cold. Here he writes much about faith alone. However, when he is under the judge, in hell, he is vile like all the rest. I have heard the judge say that when there, he is evil and is occasionally punished for his wicked deeds. It is also said that in his room the walls are bare and often made of stone, and that the room is crude and sad, and without decoration. Because of this, and whenever visitors wish to meet*

with him and speak—due to his worldwide reputation—he is too ashamed to let them enter. [...Sometimes] he is allowed to pray in his room about writing on charity and its goods, which are called good works. [28]

When the latter occurs the room is animated with decorations and flowers. But as soon as Melanchthon is left to his own devices or his own thoughts, he is no longer able to see or read the words, and what he does see, he does not understand; and then the decorations in his room vanish. The room returns to stone. It is a mirror or a reflection: a composite of the affections and thoughts that occur within it, and here I would like to recount briefly another encounter with the summerhouse.

*

I am standing in the basement at Swedenborg House, London, underneath the stage, inside an iron-doored strong room. It is bare, cold

and brick walled and I am handed a folder
with architectural drawings plus other
miscellaneous documents and artefacts. The
drawings depict multi-dimensional perspectives
of the interior of a small building in which
the front facade and floor plans are overlaid.
The hut is symmetrical. The inner dimensions
are given as 12ft x 12ft x 12ft. The distance
between the floor and rooftop ridge is the
same as that between the front door to the wall
at the rear. A subtitle to one series of black
carbon paper drawings states VICESIMUM
QUARTUM SIGNUM NOVAE HIEROSOLYMAE,
which when translated reads: TWENTY-FOUR
DESIGNS FOR THE NEW JERUSALEM. [29] But
there is an ambiguity here. The floor plans do
not make note of the dimensions of an attic nor
any of its interior details.

Delving deeper into the dossier there is also
a series of four photographs showing a hut in a
moment of repair and reconstruction. At its rear
the brickwork is exposed by clumsy repairs,

and the building's outer cladding laid bare.[30]
In another extended series of photographs the
hut is shown being delivered *en masse* from
one location to another in the Skansen open-
air park. [31] Here it has been hoisted onto a
wheeled carriage and towed between houses
and along cobbled streets. In several instances
it is squeezed between tall upright buildings,
itinerant and stripped of its fixed location.

Finally, and alongside all of this, there is a set
of black and white family photographs, one of
which is a picture of a child with blonde hair.
She is looking directly at the lens. Her family
are close by. The midday sun is shining, and
the organ is visible via a reflected interior glow.
Outside the shadows are harsh and short. [32]
Disorientated, my senses suddenly sharpen: the
design and scale of the interior room depicted
in these photographs corresponds directly to the
design and scale of my previous pencil sketch
drafted 18 months earlier when emerging from
my afternoon reverie. My visit has somehow

been prefigured. Like Melanchthon's cave, this iron-clad vault is a time vacuum. I put down the dossier and leave the room. The discovery of this folder marks my second encounter with the summerhouse. A pencil note in my diary records the date as August 1992.

S wedenborg employed two 'domestics':
Maria Norman the housekeeper and her
husband, the gardener, Nils Ahlstedt.
They were resident on the grounds when
Swedenborg arrived in 1746 and they lived in
the cottage on the property with their three
daughters aged between ten and fifteen, named
Maria, Magdalena and Catharina. [33] Robsahm
notes that it was Maria Norman who first gave
an account of Swedenborg with his eyes 'of
the brightest fire' when in conversation with
spirits, and from which he needed a moment to
compose himself. [34] It was from Maria Norman
also that we learn of the mirror once stationed
inside the summerhouse and which served

as a doorway between the worlds. Regarding the nature of these otherworldly conversations Swedenborg himself was mostly discreet but he did also, on occasion, make exceptions. For instance, when recounting the passing of his former mentor and collaborator Christopher Polhem, he writes:

> *Polhem died on Monday. He spoke with me on Thursday; and [when] invited to the funeral he saw his coffin, and those who were there, and the whole procession, and also when [he] was laid in the grave; and, in the meantime, he spoke with me, asking why they buried him when he was still alive: and also, when the priest said that he should be resuscitated at the last judgment, and yet he had been resuscitated for some time; and he marvelled that such a belief should exist, as that men should be resuscitated at the last judgment, when he was still alive; and that the body should rise again, when yet*

he himself was sensible of being in a body:
besides many other things. [35]

In another aside, and recalling the words of
Aristotle, Swedenborg notes that the great
philosopher once affirmed that one 'child' in
heaven could speak more 'in the space of half
an hour' than Aristotle himself was able to write
in 'many volumes'. [36] The reason for this is that
the speech of angels is determined exclusively
by ideas. In the highest of the heavens a single
idea holds within it an entire community of
thought and every single thought and affection
is visible and 'spreads out', radiating 'into the
communities of spirits and angels' round about
them. As a consequence, a single idea 'that goes
to make up thought contains countless facets'
and the degree to which the thought is able to
extend, so also is the degree to which a person is
able to understand and perceive. [37] By the same
token, the more material the thought the less
far it extends, and a 'closed idea' appears 'like a

black spot in which nothing else could be seen'.[38] Such is the measure of intelligence in heaven, he writes. Similarly, the degree to which a thought corresponds to any particular community of spirits or angels, to the same degree does it acquire its scale, hardness, shape, colour and size.

For Swedenborg himself however, many of his communications with the dead were heard sonorously as an 'internal dialogue' or 'inner voice'. He notes that the words or meanings drawn from such dialogues are understood universally in the next life because the language of spirits is drawn directly from the 'inner memory' and is therefore always appropriate, falling spontaneously into our 'mother tongue'. 'Souls who have entered the next life have been amazed that such a communication of another person's thoughts should exist', he adds, and that people should know 'in an instant not only the nature of another person's turn of mind but also the nature of a person's faith'.[39] Flowing with harmonious concord and cadence there is likewise no aspect of communication that does not embrace all aspects of a spirit's life.

During his lifetime there were also to emerge numerous anecdotal accounts of Swedenborg's clairvoyant capabilities, the two most famous involving Swedenborg having witnessed the burning of Stockholm whilst having dinner in Gothenburg and a conversation with Queen Louisa Ulrika who sought counsel with Swedenborg regarding her recently deceased brother, Prince Augustus William of Prussia. But this aspect of his special gift would soon become a curse. News spread and earthly visitors began convening on Hornsgatan, seeking information on recently deceased relatives and other matters. And it is here, interestingly, that the philosopher Immanuel Kant enters the scene.

'The portrait of this man [Swedenborg] is remarkable but time fails me to describe it', he writes in a letter to the Prussian socialite Charlotte von Knobloch dated sometime between 1758 and 1764. 'How I wish that I might have questioned this remarkable man myself [...] I await with longing the book that Swedenborg is about to publish in London. I have made every provision for receiving it as soon as it shall leave the press'.[40]

It is via Kant in fact that we have a detailed description of the incident of Swedenborg communicating with spirits about a missing receipt and the great fire of Stockholm, and it was from Kant that we learn of Queen Louisa Ulrika's desire to speak with her deceased brother, Prince Augustus William of Prussia. But Kant's interest was not to last. In 1766 and sensing an incompatibility with his own developing critical philosophy, he published his now infamous *Dreams of a Spirit-Seer* where he describes the writing of Swedenborg as 'the wild chimeras of this worst of all dreamers' and of Swedenborg's greatest work, *Arcana Caelestia*, as 'eight volumes quarto full of nonsense'. But his reading of Swedenborg is also acutely detailed. 'The language of spirits is an immediate communication of ideas', he notes, referring to an obscure passage deep in Swedenborg's system, 'but it is always connected with the appearance of that language which the observer ordinarily speaks [...Hence a] spirit reads in the memory of another spirit the ideas which are contained in the inner memory with clearness'. [41] We also find in Kant's critical philosophy an elaboration on the nature of space and time that bears a remarkable resemblance to Swedenborg's own philosophic system. Space and time are internal states, writes Swedenborg, a priori conditions of thought that we impose upon the world.

Another theme drawn out by Kant, and which bears scrutiny within his later critical philosophy, is the claim that for Swedenborg, 'corporeal beings have no substance of their own', i.e., they exist only via a priori principles that give cause to them. It is for this reason, Kant adds, citing Swedenborg, that 'our knowledge of material things has a double significance', an external meaning that is linked to the inter-relations of matter and an internal meaning related to inner principles. In this way, objects and things conform to material laws but only insofar as these laws correspond with the inner principles that provide them with their 'form, activity and stability'. By and large, he adds, this inner meaning is unknown but it can nevertheless be intuited via a symbolic interplay of 'images' with our 'interior spiritual' states. Thus objects or phenomena are essentially 'appearances' and 'he [Swedenborg] can talk about gardens, vast countries, dwelling places, galleries and arcades' as being representative of spiritual causes. In this way, and momentarily, Kant opened a central connection between Swedenborg's system and his own later epistemology. But then just as quickly he moves away or recoils with a sense of horror. 'If metaphysics is the science of the boundaries of human reason' he notes, then we must 'retire with some confusion from a foolish attempt,' and seek again 'the ground of experience and common sense'. [42]

S wedenborg left his property in Stockholm for the last time in July, 1770.[43] He arrived in Amsterdam soon after to publish his final theological work *The True Christian Religion*—with his long-term associates François Changuion and Christian Sepp—and then moved on to London. He made ready one final work which became lost. In his final months he suffered temporarily from a stroke, and then at the lodgings of Richard Shearsmith in Cold Bath Fields he passed into the next world, having predicted the time and date of his death. His sparse belongings were gathered by his friend Charles Lindegren and sent back to Sweden with the

message that they were not of 'much value'
but are gathered 'because he thought the
family would wish to own something that the
worthy man had worn'. [44] The main house and
property were put up for auction. [45]

Shortly after the sale, the estate was divided
into three separate lots and the summerhouse
initially became used for a variety of diverse
ends including a shed for storage, a residence
for a family on low income and on another
occasion as a hideout for a gang of thieves. [46]
By the early 1890s the summerhouse had
changed hands once again and following
local fears of hauntings, the main house was
pulled down in 1888 and the summerhouse fell
into the possession of a stone carver, Richard
Sundell. Having installed a life-size waxwork of
Swedenborg in a coffin, with the internal walls
decorated from 'floor to ceiling' with 'black
cloth covered with silver stars', he introduced
an entrance fee of 10 ore. 'In the middle of the
room', writes one visitor,

*stands a catafalque, and on this a coffin
containing an effigy of Swedenborg. The
head is made of plaster, and is said to be a
good likeness, even the death pallor having
been reproduced. Some antique candelabra
with wax candles are placed on each side
of the catafalque to make the whole more
impressive.* [47]

A similar account was printed four years later in
the Swedenborgian periodical *New Church Life*
where the hut is described as being surrounded
on 'three sides by shanties and houses'.

'Interiorly it is even more disappointing', the
writer adds,

*owing to the greed, bad taste, and sickly
sentimentality of some 'enterprising'
speculator, who has draped the square
room with crêpe and silver stars, and in the
midst has placed a catafalque, containing
a wax figure representing the dead body of*

*Swedenborg, lying in state, with a bunch of
white wax flowers in his hand. (Entrance
fee, 25 ore.)* [48]

Confirmation of this description is found in two
photographs of the period, a copy of the first
being an image I am handed later by my guide
at Skansen, and in another, from the outside,
a picture of Sundell himself under a sign
announcing the entrance fee.

It was under these conditions, in 1896, that
the hut was purchased by Artur Hazelius, the son
of a Swedenborgian, for 500 kronor from Mrs H
Ahlström and moved to the Skansen open-air
park, where it now resides. Transported in one
piece, the hut was restored and a medallion was
cast. An 1895 letter to Hazelius from Ahlström,
reveals that she offered to sell the summerhouse
to him for 1500 kronor. [49] Other records show
that the price was negotiated down to 500
kronor, which was paid for with the help of the
descendants of the anti-slavery activist August

Nordenskjöld. It was August Nordenskjöld, in trun, who had arranged for the binding of the 114 separate Swedenborg codices found in the summerhouse attic. [50]

Now bound in white vellum, these codices are stored on two shelves in the archive at the Swedish Academy of Sciences and have since been awarded UNESCO world memory status. On my own first visit to Stockholm and the Academy in 1996 I head straight for these manuscript volumes and find a small drawing of a hut with an arched roof. It is a dwelling that Swedenborg is said to have witnessed and sketched when visiting an alien planet in the spiritual world. Swedenborg describes the building as a communal space, but it is also diaphanous and responsive: it contracts and expands to the thoughts and affections of those within. There is also suggested here another connection which is more difficult to formulate. It is linked to a set of relations giving form to an internal locus: 'Every state has its own location', writes Swedenborg, [51] and the movement between places and space, is nothing other than the movement between states.

In the Academy archive I am also handed a 16-page brochure containing an auction catalogue of the summerhouse library. The catalogue contains nearly 400 titles related to physics, chemistry, mathematics, mineralogy, geology, history, theology, philosophy and anatomy. Also listed are four Hebrew Bibles, seven Latin Bibles, three Greek New Testaments and a Bible in English plus multiple other miscellaneous works including an English edition of the *Book of Common Prayer*, Henry Venn's *The Complete Duty of Man*, Newton's *Philosophiae Naturalis Principia Mathematica*, Hugo Grotius' *De veritate religionis Christianae* and several works by his cousin Carl Linnaeus. Over 70 titles are dated post-1746, meaning they were purchased or received by Swedenborg after having set up home in the summerhouse. Almost half of the titles are printed in German and Swedish, with the remaining in Hebrew, Greek, Latin, Dutch, Italian and English. I am particularly struck by the presence of G A Reeves's *A New History of London* and a German edition of George Berkeley's *Siris*.

The catalogue itself is divided into nine sections arranged according to folios, quartos, octavos and duodecimos, and corresponding neatly to the nine spheres or societies in the next life and the spirits and inhabitants that Swedenborg met there. These spirits, in turn, have their own libraries. Of these Swedenborg writes that there are books 'written by correspondences' by members of the 'Ancient Churches' and, still further in the interior, books for the even more Ancient:

> *There was a vast number who studied the books, some of whom became learned, many intelligent and others wise. There also appeared places or chambers even more interior and whose libraries became brighter*

and brighter. To myself and others, however they appeared in a dimmer light, because we were incapable of penetrating those depths of wisdom which are there; and, besides, those who are in exteriors are not allowed to enter into the interior parts for various reasons. The places in these libraries were divided into many [repositories], according to the faculties of those who studied. [52]

Following this, I now feel ready for my third encounter with the summerhouse and my first visit in person.

*

I arrive early. It is cold. A sharp, crisp winter morning and the front doors are locked. Waiting for my Skansen guide, I press my nose against the front window. Inside a cluster of stone cherubs are randomly placed. A ray of sunlight passes across the front facade, and for a moment there is a realignment of external and

internal ratios: the inside seems bigger than the
outside. I imagine where the straw bed may
once have rested, and the possible placement
of Swedenborg's desk and chair. There is no
veil in front of the internal doors as seen in my
dream, and no internal voice. But I am joined by
a peacock on the front step and a herd of ducks
are roaming close by.

I have with me a Polaroid instamatic camera.
I document the front eaves of the pavilion-
roof now covered with timber slats. At the top
is the cupola with windows on three sides.
I document the window frames and door. A
tourist notice board explains that the house
'was built in the 1740s' and 'played a vital
part in his spiritual life'. I document the stone
steps and the concrete base below which
Swedenborg had once excavated a cellar. Aide
memoirs perhaps, but not quite. It is four years
since my oneiric awakening and I now see
clearly what my dream and the photographs
at Swedenborg House had only suggested.

The hut is a staging post or model for the New Jerusalem in its most elemental form: an *interregnum*.

Eventually my Skansen guide arrives. She is dressed in period costume and hands me a photocopy, an image of a coffin with a wax figure of Swedenborg. She speaks briefly of Swedenborg's life, and the angelic presences within the hut, but my focus is drawn to the peacock and the stone cherubs from the garden. I am reminded that within Swedenborg's system of correspondences a peacock signifies the adornment of spiritual things whilst cherubs signify the good of angelic love. My guide fumbles with the keys and eventually the outer doors are unlocked. Peeking inside I see the inner door ajar. We hesitate at the threshold, and then we enter.

Visitors to the summerhouse today
are met with a clean empty space
standing isolated in the rose garden
on the west side of Skansen. Behind the
interior double doors the recess at the rear
is bare, and depending on the needs of the
Skansen museum, it is otherwise unoccupied
but may occasionally house ornaments from
the garden or a table with chairs. The exterior
is painted a muted yellow with grey and brown
detailing, and the interior is layered with a green
wallpaper on which are stained the darkened
outline of absent framed portraits. The wood
burning stove is gone, and the ladder leading
to the attic. Absent also is the annexe that once

held the library and the shed that held the
garden tools. Of the few photographs still extant
of the summerhouse in situ at Hornsgatan, a
number comprise a series of black and white
pictures taken around 1876, attributed to
photographer Du Jardin. In these daguerreotypes
one can still glimpse the covered walkway
extending back to the main house which enabled
Swedenborg to have access in all weathers and at
any time of the day or night. A late arrival, and
once stationed in the sitting room of the main
house, is a small hand-painted grey organ, once
owned by Swedenborg himself.

In my own private collection, I now have
over 200 Polaroid images of the hut. They are
detailed and comprehensive but also acutely
posthumous. The scene of writing, or the scene
of visions, has long since fled: what remains
is a remnant or trace. The ratios of the room
need to be re-internalized. Of the hut's interior
decor, the glazing above the inner door is intact,
and the two side facade windows have been

reinstated. The attic remains undisturbed, and one can see the repaired hole in the roof tiling where the chimney from the stove would once have extended. The door frame to the library is present but is cased-in from the outside. At Swedenborg House in London, in the basement vault formerly mentioned, there is still held a small fragment of bark taken from the poplar tree at the front of the summerhouse. At the Academy of the New Church in the US there is likewise a small cutting of the hessian that once lined its internal walls, which pre-dates the invention of printed mass-produced wallpaper. In Berkeley, California Swedenborg's desk lamps are kept, which he would have used during the long winter nights when working 'without much regard to the distinction of day and night' and having no 'fixed time for labour or rest'.[53] This description also aligns closely with Swedenborg's observations on the relationship between the circular times of the day and the four cardinal points of the compass.

In Hornsgatan, on the site of Swedenborg's property, the summerhouse faced east towards the rising sun. Today, in contrast, on the island of Djurgården it faces north, and access is gained from the central pathway from the south. Angels, like people 'turn and move their faces and bodies in every direction', writes Swedenborg, 'yet they have east always in front of their eyes'. The reason for this he adds is that in heaven the 'common centre' is 'the Lord' who is seen by them 'as a Sun' in the east. [54] The west therefore is at their back, the 'south is at [their] right, the north at [their] left'. [55] For this reason, in heaven, it is generally not possible to see the back of another's head. For spirits more commonly, the shifting nature of their ruling love is reflected in the shifting orientation of their relationship with these cardinal points and the type of thinking or thoughts available to them. The further a spirit moves east, the greater they are immersed in love, and the closer they move to the south the more they are immersed in truth. Something similar is also encountered in the varying times of the day. Dawn 'corresponds to the coming and presence of the Lord, which takes place when an angel enters a state of peace, innocence, and heavenly love, and consequently has a feeling of joy'. [56] Midnight in contrast is reserved exclusively for the fallen or the lost. It represents the absence of truth and the loss of innocence.

*

In closing, I would like to draw attention to one final image, related to the idea of orientation in conjunction with Swedenborg's vast and shifting otherworld architectonic. Following a visit to the summerhouse in 2008, and when accepting his Nobel Prize for Literature, the great French/ Mauritian writer J M G Le Clézio spoke of the powerful vibration one senses in the 'poetry of Jalal ad-Din Rumi' and in the

visionary architecture of Emanuel

Swedenborg. The shiver one feels on reading the most beautiful texts of humankind, such as the speech that Chief Stealth gave in the mid-19th century to the President of the United States upon conceding his land: 'We may be brothers after all...' [57]

And within this vibration—which for Le Clézio 'exists in language alone'—there is encountered something of 'silence', of 'mockery' and also 'of paradise': a greatness as 'impalpable as the wind, ethereal as the clouds, infinite as the sea' and which emerges in vertical motion as a direct response or reflection of Baudelaire's 'Correspondances' and its forest of symbols.

Indeed. And the language here is rich: it chimes closely with Le Clézio's own poetics of place. But there is something more elemental implied in Swedenborg's correspondences that is only hinted at by Baudelaire and Le Clézio, and which gains fuller poetic expression or understanding in the vast mythic constructions

of William Blake and the intimate poetry of
W B Yeats.

In Swedenborg's visionary architecture, with
its endless fluctuations and affiliations, there
is assembled a framework of discrete degrees
wherein language and thought are overlaid
in an ever-increasing spiral that expands
simultaneously in all directions.

The speech of angels is like the thought
of spirits, and the speech of spirits is like the
thought of people and each of these thoughts,
when expressed, takes the form of a visible
representation, writes Swedenborg. Such spirals
or circumrotations are shown in configurations
that are indefinitely perfect, and when thoughts
and affections circulate accordingly, they arrive
naturally into a pattern like the unfolding grey
matter in the brain. [58]

In this way our ideas move and bend in
mosaics that transcend even the understanding
of angels, and travel at great distances in an
instant. Hence, in the final reckoning, when

place is revealed as an attribute of thought,
time and space are dissolved, subsumed to an
untraceable movement of intangible gyrations.

Endnotes

1   Gaston Bachelard, *The Poetics of Space*, tr. Maria
    Jolas (London: Penguin, 2014), p. 21.

2   Seamus Heaney, *The Place of Writing* in *Finders
    Keepers: Selected Prose 1971-2001* (London: Faber &
    Faber, 2003), p. 235.

3   Ibid., pp. 234-5.

4   Simon Unwin, *Twenty Buildings Every Architect
    Should Understand* (London: Routledge, 2010), p. 93.

5   William Blake, *A Vision: The Inspiration of the Poet*,
    drawing and watercolour on paper, *c*. 1819-20, Tate
    Gallery.

6   Swedenborg, *Index Biblicus* (Codex 6), MS
    Swedenborg 125:1, in the Emanuel Swedenborg
    Collection at the Royal Swedish Academy of Science,
    Center for History of Science [translation by SM].
    A reproduction of the manuscript can be found

in Swedenborg, *Index Biblicus*, vol. 1 (Holmiae: Officina Phototypographica Lagrelius & Westphal, 1916), p. 533.

7   Ibid., p. 357.

8   Alfred Action (tr. and ed.), *The Letters and Memorials of Emanuel Swedenborg*, 2 vols. (Bryn Athyn, PA: Swedenborg Scientific Association, 1948-55), vol. 1, p. 503.

9   Swedenborg, *Autographa*, Tomus X, *Arcana Coelestia*, vol. I (Holmiae: Officina Phototypographica Lagrelius & Westphal, 1916), p. 487. The draft of this part of the manuscript of *Arcana Coelestia* is dated *c*. 1751, but Swedenborg frequently reused his notebooks and his memorandum on building materials for the summerhouse is likely from an earlier date.

10 See 'Description of the Late Assessor, Mr Emanuel Swedenborg's estate at Södermalm', in *Swedenborg's Lusthus*, ed. Stephen McNeilly (London: Swedenborg Society, 2024), pp. 273-8.

11 'Swedenborg and His Gardener-Folks', in R L Tafel (tr., ed. and comp.), *Documents Concerning the Life and Character of Emanuel Swedenborg*, 3 vols. (London: Swedenborg Society, 1875-7), vol. II:2, doc. no. 292, p. 734.

12 Swedenborg, *The Spiritual Diary*, vol. 3, tr. George

Bush and John H Smithson (London: Swedenborg Society, 2003), §4142, p. 306.

13 Swedenborg, *Arcana Caelestia*, tr. John Elliott, 12 vols. (London: Swedenborg Society, 1983-99), vol. 1, §870, p. 333.

14 Ibid., §100, p. 45.

15 Swedenborg, *Divine, Love and Wisdom*, tr. Clifford Harley & Doris H Harley (London: Swedenborg Society, 1987), §408, p. 186.

16 F G Lindh, 'Swedenborg som Söderbo', in *Nya Kyrkans Tidning*, vol. 46. nos. 22-23 (November-December 1921), pp. 169-72.

17 Acton (tr. and ed.), *Letters and Memorials of Emanuel Swedenborg*, vol. 1, pp. 490-1.

18 Swedenborg, *The Animal Kingdom*, tr. J J G Wilkinson, 2 vols. (London: W Newbery, 1843-4), vol. I, §16, p. 11.

19 Swedenborg, *Swedenborg's Journal of Dreams 1743-1744*, tr. J J G Wilkinson, ed. William Ross Woofenden, 2nd edn. (London: Swedenborg Society and Bryn Athyn, PA: Swedenborg Scientific Association, 1989), pp. 21-23.

20 Carl Robsahm, *Memoirs of Swedenborg and Other Documents*, tr. Anders Hallengren, ed. Stephen McNeilly (London: Swedenborg Society, 2011), pp. 6-7.

21 Acton (tr. and ed.), *Letters and Memorials of Emanuel Swedenborg*, vol. 2, pp. 510-13.

22 Swedenborg, *A Hieroglyphic Key to Natural and Spiritual Arcana (1744)*, in *Psychological Transactions*, tr. Alfred Acton, 2nd edn. (Bryn Athyn, PA: Swedenborg Scientific Association, 1984), p. 193. Translation revised by SM.

23 Swedenborg, *Arcana Caelestia*, vol. 2, see §1376. Translation revised by SM.

24 Swedenborg, *The Spiritual Diary*, vol. V, tr. James F Buss (London: James Speirs, 1902), §5991, p. 141.

25 Swedenborg, *The Spiritual Diary*, vol. III, tr. George Bush and John H Smithson (London: James Speirs, 1883), §3605, pp. 126-7. Translation revised by SM.

26 Ibid., p. 127.

27 Swedenborg, *Arcana Caelestia*, vol. 2, §1629, p. 215.

28 Swedenborg, *The Last Judgment (Posthumous)* (London: Swedenborg Society, 1934), §§27-28. Translation by SM.

29 Included in the exhibition *Swedenborg's Lusthus*, Swedenborg House, curated by Stephen McNeilly (London, 2024).

30 See 'Miscellaneous Iconography', in *Swedenborg's Lusthus*, ed. Stephen McNeilly (London: Swedenborg Society, 2024), p. 261.

31 See Arne Biörnstad, 'Swedenborg's Lusthus being

moved from its old location behind Bergsman's Garden to the Rose Garden March 1964', in *Swedenborg's Lusthus*, ed. Stephen McNeilly (London: Swedenborg Society, 2024), pp. 185-208.

32 Included in the exhibition *Swedenborg's Lusthus*, Swedenborg House, curated by Stephen McNeilly (London, 2024).

33 Henrik Alm, 'Emanuel Swedenborgs Hus och Trädgård' (Emanuel Swedenborg's House and Garden), in *Samfundet Sankt Eriks Årsbok 1938* (*Yearbook of the Association of Saint Erik, 1938*) (Stockholm: Kgl. Boktr. P A Norstedt & Söner, 1938), pp. 169-70.

34 Robsahm, *Memoirs of Swedenborg and Other Documents*, p. 13.

35 Swedenborg, *The Spiritual Diary*, vol. IV, tr. George Bush and James F Buss (London: James Speirs, 1889), §4752m, p. 70.

36 Swedenborg, *The Spiritual Diary*, vol. III, §3950, p. 241.

37 Swedenborg, *Arcana Caelestia*, vol. 9, §6599, p. 400.

38 Ibid., §6620, p. 408.

39 Ibid., vol. 2, §1637, p. 218 and §1389, p. 113.

40 Immanuel Kant, 'Letter on Swedenborg to Charlotte von Knobloch', in *Dreams of a Spirit-Seer*, tr. Emanuel F Goerwitz, ed. Frank Sewall (London:

New Church Press, 1915), Annexe II, p. 159.

41 Kant, *Dreams of a Spirit-Seer*, pp. 111, 101 and 105.

42 Ibid., pp. 112-14.

43 Acton, *Letters and Memorials of Emanuel Swedenborg*, vol. 2, p. 734.

44 Cyriel Odhner Sigstedt, *The Swedenborg Epic* (London: Swedenborg Society, 1981), pp. 431, 435 (quote on p. 435).

45 The house and garden were purchased by Swedenborg's nephew Bishop Lars Benzelstjerna for an undisclosed sum. Lars's son, Carl Benzelstjerna, was responsible for transferring the care of Swedenborg's manuscripts—kept in the loft of the *lusthus*—to the Swedish Academy of Sciences, where they still remain. See C Th. Odhner, *Annals Of The New Church* (Philadelpia: Academy of the New Church, 1898), p. 107 and R L Tafel (tr., ed. and comp.), *Documents*, vol. II:2, p. 1251.

46 Ed Gyllenhaal, 'An 1896 Medal Commemorates the Moving of His "Summerhouse"', in *Glencairn Museum News*, vol. 24, no. 2 (2002), pp. 4-6.

47 'Notes and Reviews', in *New Church Life*, vol. XI, no. 12 (December 1891), p. 226.

48 C Th. Odhner, 'Professor Odhner's Visit to England and Sweden', in *New Church Life*, vol. XV, no. 12 (December 1895), p. 187.

49 See H Ahlström to A Hazelius, Stockholm, 14/10/1895. Skansen archives, Stockholm.

50 S C Eby, *The Story of Swedenborg's Manuscripts* (New York: New Church Press, 1926), p. 24.

51 Swedenborg, *Spiritual Experiences*, vol. 3, tr. J Durban Odhner (Bryn Athyn, PA: General Church of the New Jerusalem, 2003), §4403.2, p. 365.

52 Swedenborg, *Spiritual Diary*, vol. V, §5999, pp. 145-6. Translation revised by SM.

53 Robsahm, quoted in R L Tafel (tr., ed. and comp.), *Documents*, vol. I, p. 32.

54 Swedenborg, *Heaven and Hell*, tr. Doris H Harley (London: Swedenborg Society, 1992), §143, p. 72.

55 Ibid., §144, p. 73.

56 Swedenborg, *Arcana Caelestia*, vol. 11, §9387, p. 230.

57 J M G Le Clézio, 'In the forest of paradoxes', Nobel Lecture, 7 December 2008, at <<https://www.nobelprize.org/prizes/literature/2008/clezio/lecture>>, accessed 30 November 2023.

58 Swedenborg, *Arcana Caelestia*, vol. 8, see §§6607, p. 404.